William J. Clinton

WILLIAM J. *Clinton*

OUR FORTY-SECOND PRESIDENT

By Ann Graham Gaines

SPIRIT
of America™

The Child's World®, *Inc.*
Chanhassen, Minnesota

WILLIAM J. *Clinton*

Published in the United States of America by The Child's World®, Inc.
PO Box 326 • Chanhassen, MN 55317-0326 • 800-599-READ • www.childsworld.com

Acknowledgments
    The Creative Spark: Mary Francis-DeMarois, Project Director; Elizabeth Sirimarco Budd, Series Editor;
    Robert Court, Design and Art Direction; Janine Graham, Page Layout; Jennifer Moyers, Production

    The Child's World®, Inc.: Mary Berendes, Publishing Director; Red Line Editorial, Fact Research;
    Cindy Klingel, Curriculum Advisor; Robert Noyed, Historical Advisor

Photos
    Cover: White House Collection, courtesy White House Historical Association; courtesy of the Clinton
    Birthplace: 6-8, 11; Corbis: 20, 21, 22, 23, 24, 25, 27, 31, 32, 33, 35, 36, 37; Courtesy of Georgetown
    University 12-14; Courtesy of the Jimmy Carter Library: 18; Library of Congress 9, 10, 23, 29;
    Courtesy of the Wellesley College Archives: 16, 19

Registration
    The Child's World®, Inc., Spirit of America™, and their associated logos are the sole property and
    registered trademarks of The Child's World®, Inc.

Library of Congress Cataloging-in-Publication Data
    Gaines, Ann.
      William J. Clinton : our forty-second president / by Ann Graham Gaines.
        p. cm.
      Includes bibliographical references (p.   ) and index.
      ISBN 1-56766-876-3 (library bound : alk. paper)
      1. Clinton, Bill, 1946–   .—Juvenile literature. 2. Presidents—United
    States—Biography—Juvenile literature. [1. Clinton, Bill, 1946–   . 2. Presidents.]   I. Title.
      E886 .G34 2001
      973.929'092—dc21
                                                                              2001000410

20 24 33

Contents

Chapter ONE

Arkansas Childhood

Bill Clinton, the 42nd U.S. president, did not have an easy childhood. His father died three months before he was born, and the family never had much money. Bill was determined to succeed, however, and worked hard to achieve his goals.

WILLIAM (BILL) CLINTON, PRESIDENT OF THE United States from 1993 until 2001, had many problems. He was accused of wrongdoing on several occasions. Even so, he remained popular and accomplished many of his goals as president. During his time in office, the United States was, for many people, a successful and happy place to live. Although most Americans did not like certain things Clinton did, others considered him the greatest **politician** of his generation.

Clinton's name was William Jefferson Blythe when he was born in Hope, Arkansas, on August 19, 1946. He was the son of Virginia and Bill Blythe. Sadly, the child who grew up to be the nation's 42nd president never knew his father. Bill Blythe died in a car accident before his son was born.

Bill spent the first years of his life living at his grandparents' home (right) in Hope, Arkansas. His mother returned to school to study advanced nursing, so his grandparents took care of him.

After her husband died, Virginia Blythe stayed with her parents. Three months later, her baby was born. She named him William Jefferson Blythe, after his father, and nick-named him "Billy." When Billy was still very small, Virginia asked her parents to take care of him. She wanted to return to nursing school to learn new skills. She studied the science of how to put patients to sleep so they could have surgery. These special skills would mean she could earn more money. Virginia knew she would need it to raise Billy by herself. Even so, this was a difficult decision. She and her son would be apart for two years while she completed her studies.

Growing up, Billy Clinton was a friendly, outgoing boy. He is shown here on his third birthday.

Interesting Facts

▸ Bill Clinton's grandparents were not well educated, but they knew the importance of learning. They taught Bill to count and read at a young age. In first grade, he was already reading the newspaper.

Virginia finished school in 1950. That same year, she remarried. Her new husband was a car salesman named Roger Clinton. Unfortunately, their marriage would be an unhappy one. Roger was an angry man who drank too much. Even so, Bill used "Clinton" as his last name once he started school. No matter how difficult his stepfather could be, Bill didn't feel sorry for himself. "It made me a lot more self-reliant and tougher than I might have been," he later remembered.

When Bill was seven years old, the family moved to Hot Springs, Arkansas. Three years later, Bill's brother, Roger, was born. Bill vowed to protect his brother, both from their angry father and from any other problems he might face. Virginia Clinton took good care of both her sons. She and her parents made sure the boys studied but also found time for fun. Unfortunately, Arkansas's schools were among the worst in the country. For one thing, the state did not require its teachers to have college degrees. Virginia Clinton often complained about the schools her sons attended. Bill remembered this later in life. Improving education in both Arkansas and in the United States would be one of his major goals as a government leader.

By the time he entered high school, Bill Clinton was active and popular. His classmates elected him class president. He played in the school band as well. During the summer of 1963, teachers at his high school selected Bill to go to Arkansas Boys State. The American Legion sponsors this special camp every year in all 50 states. Boys who attend learn about the government and hold their own elections. The other boys elected Bill a senator. With other Boys State senators from all over the country, he traveled to Washington, D.C.,

This family portrait shows Bill (right) with his brother, Roger, and their mother. The three of them tried to have a happy family life, although their household was often troubled by Bill's unkind and abusive stepfather.

As a young man, Bill was very smart and did well in school. He loved music and played the saxophone. In fact, he was a leader in the high school band and even played with a jazz trio called the Three Blind Mice.

to participate in Boys Nation. There the boys split into **political parties.** They discussed the important issues of the day. They also went on tours, visiting the Capitol, the Library of Congress, and other historic landmarks.

July 24, 1963, was the highlight of Bill's week at Boys Nation. All the boys were invited to the White House to meet President John F. Kennedy. Bill Clinton made sure he was the first in line to shake President Kennedy's hand.

Most people in Bill's hometown belonged to the Republican Party, one of the two most powerful political parties in the United States. But Bill preferred the ideas of the other major party, the Democratic Party. Kennedy was a Democrat—and Bill's hero. Bill admired the way Kennedy wanted to help all Americans, rich and poor, black and white. Before meeting the president, Bill had told his friends he might grow up to become a doctor, a reporter, or a musician. But after attending Boys Nation, he returned to Arkansas with a new dream. "When I went home, I had the feeling that if I worked hard and prepared myself, I could have an impact," he later recalled. Bill Clinton had decided to become a politician.

All his life, Bill Clinton would treasure this photograph, which was taken when he had the chance to meet President John F. Kennedy. Today Kennedy is still one of Clinton's personal heroes.

Chapter TWO

The Young Politician

When it was time to pick a college, Clinton's excellent grades allowed him to choose from the nation's best schools. He chose to attend Georgetown University.

BILL CLINTON GRADUATED FROM HIGH school in 1964 and looked forward to college. He decided to attend Georgetown University because it was located in Washington, D.C. Politics fascinated him, and he wanted to live in the nation's capital city—the heart of American political life. While at Georgetown, Clinton was popular and busy, just as he had been at home. His classmates thought he was bright, funny, and friendly, and he was elected president of his class. Attending Georgetown was expensive, but his good grades earned him scholarships to help him pay for college.

In the summer of 1966, Clinton returned to Arkansas for his summer vacation. There he took part in his first political **campaign,** working for Judge Frank Holt. Judge Holt was running for governor of Arkansas. During Holt's campaign, Clinton practiced public speaking. Holt lost the election, but Clinton's work paid off in another way. Holt helped Clinton find a part-time job back in Washington. Soon he would be working for William Fulbright, one of the two senators from Arkansas.

A REALISTIC APPROACH TO STUDENT GOVERNMENT

BILL CLINTON

CANDIDATE

PRESIDENT OF THE STUDENT COUNCIL

Fulbright was chairman of the Senate's foreign relations committee. He hired Clinton as an aide. In this job, Clinton did small tasks, such as sorting mail, clipping articles from newspapers, and filing papers. But it offered him an important opportunity to learn about the nation's dealings with other countries.

At the time, the United States was involved in the Vietnam War. Thousands of young American men were being **drafted** into the military. They were sent overseas to fight in

Clinton kept very busy during his college years. He was president of his class and took jobs to help pay for school. He also worked as a volunteer in a student clinic. Even with all these activities, Clinton managed to keep good grades.

13

Clinton won a Rhodes Scholarship in 1968, his senior year at Georgetown University. This award gave him the opportunity to study in England for two years.

the war, and many of them lost their lives. Fulbright firmly believed that the United States should withdraw from the Vietnam War. His opinion had a strong effect on Clinton. As a student, Clinton was fortunate—he could avoid the draft. Still, he did not want the United States to send any more American men to fight in a faraway country.

In 1968, during his final year in college, Clinton won a Rhodes Scholarship. This important award is given to outstanding students who also are campus leaders and athletes. (Clinton was chairman of Georgetown's Student Athletic Commission.) Students who win the scholarship continue their studies at England's Oxford University.

Clinton returned from England in 1970 and enrolled at Yale Law School. Yale is among the best schools in the nation. He wanted to go there to continue his excellent education. He also knew that attending Yale would help him meet powerful people. Knowing the right people could help him become a successful politician.

While at Yale, Clinton worked on a Senate campaign. He also worked for the Democratic Party's presidential **candidate,** George McGovern. Students around the country supported McGovern because he wanted Americans to withdraw from Vietnam. Clinton managed McGovern's campaign in Texas. This was a big responsibility for Clinton, because he had to manage a large amount of money. He also organized the efforts of hundreds of volunteers. McGovern lost the election, but Clinton gained important experience from the campaign.

While at law school, Clinton began to date another student, Hillary Rodham. Like Clinton, she was hardworking and wanted to achieve great things in life. They liked each other immediately. Clinton graduated with a law degree in 1973. Rodham stayed at Yale longer than he did, but their friendship continued.

After law school, Clinton returned home to Arkansas. He took a job as a professor of law at the University of Arkansas in Fayetteville. The following year, in 1974, Clinton felt he was ready to run for office. He entered the election for the U.S. House of Representatives. He lost to John Paul Hammerschmidt, the **incumbent,** but the race was close. Clinton remained popular among Arkansas Democrats.

Hillary Rodham had moved to Arkansas to help with Clinton's campaign.

Clinton met Hillary Rodham while studying at Yale Law School. The two were fond of each other from the start. After dating for several years, they married in October of 1975.

She also worked as a law professor at the University of Arkansas. On October 11, 1975, the couple married. The next year, she worked to help Clinton in another election. He was running for attorney general of Arkansas. An attorney general is the chief lawyer who works for a state or national government.

After winning the election, the Clintons moved to Little Rock, the capital of Arkansas. Hillary went to work for a law firm. As attorney general, Clinton's number-one goal was to help the people in his state. He created a new state office to make sure utility companies **conserved** energy. He also appeared in court to argue against the phone company's plan to increase its rates. During this time, he was able to meet important leaders in Washington. President Jimmy Carter invited the Clintons to dinner at the White House. Clinton also met with other leaders in Washington, where he talked about issues such as protecting the environment and conserving energy.

In 1978, Clinton was ready to try for a more powerful office. He ran for governor of Arkansas and won. Governor Clinton entered

While Clinton ran in the election for attorney general of Arkansas, he and Hillary also campaigned for the Democratic presidential candidate, Jimmy Carter. Carter won his election, and Clinton was invited to meet with him at the White House.

office brimming with ideas. First of all, he hoped to improve the state's schools. Education had made a big difference in his life, and he wanted more young people to have the same opportunities. Clinton also wanted to create a new energy department. Its job would be to find better ways to use and conserve energy. He hoped to improve health care in Arkansas as well.

18

Unfortunately, Clinton ran into problems. The nation was in a recession. During a recession, prices rise, and many people lose their jobs or cannot find work. Like other states, Arkansas had money problems. The state government couldn't pay for all of Clinton's programs. When he couldn't accomplish his goals, Clinton's popularity began to decline.

The Clintons have always been very supportive of each other's goals. Hillary supported Bill in all of his political activities. At the same time, she was a very successful lawyer with a busy career.

▶ In the early 1970s, President Richard Nixon was accused of wrongdoing. Congress formed a special committee to investigate the matter, which became known as the Watergate **scandal.** After graduating from Yale, Bill Clinton and Hillary Rodham were both offered jobs with this congressional committee. Hillary accepted the position, but Bill decided to return to Arkansas, where he became a law professor.

▶ As early as 1977, Bill Clinton showed his commitment to protecting the environment. As attorney general of Arkansas, he fought against the construction of a coal-burning factory, which would have polluted the air.

Clinton was 32 years old when he became the governor of Arkansas. At that time, he was the youngest governor in the country.

20

BILL CLINTON GREW UP DURING A DIFFICULT time in American history. While he was a teenager, the United States had entered the Vietnam War. **Communists** had taken over the country of North Vietnam. Then they invaded South Vietnam. First France and then the United States helped South Vietnam fight back against the invaders.

Americans argued about the war. Many believed communism was dangerous. They wanted the United States to fight against this system of government wherever it occurred. Other Americans protested against U.S. involvement in the war. As time went by, the army drafted thousands of young Americans to fight in Vietnam. Many died there. Others returned from the war wounded and mentally scarred.

As young men, Bill Clinton and his friends knew that they might be drafted. Like many other young Americans, Clinton did not like the war, and he did not want to fight. In 1969, he was drafted. The rules had changed, and some students could be drafted by then. After he received his draft notice, Clinton enrolled at the University of Alabama Law School. Then he joined the university's ROTC (which stands for Reserve Officer Training Corps). The ROTC prepares students to join the military after college. Joining this group meant that Clinton would not be sent to fight overseas. But that fall, Clinton did not go to law school. He returned to England instead. By that time, it had become clear that the army would soon stop drafting soldiers. Questions of how Clinton had avoided the draft arose later in his political career. Some people believed he was wrong not to fight for his country.

Chapter THREE

President Clinton

Clinton was not reelected governor in 1980, but two years later, he returned to office. He was governor of Arkansas from 1982 through 1992.

IN THE FALL OF 1980, BILL CLINTON RAN FOR reelection as governor but lost. He was just 34 years old. Some people wondered whether his political career had ended. Clinton went back to working as a lawyer, but he had already decided to run for governor again in 1982. He traveled all over the state, giving speeches to the many groups that invited him. He also met with people who had helped him in earlier elections. Clinton was elected governor again in 1982—and then in 1984, 1986, and 1990. (In 1986, the Arkansas governor's term was changed from two years to four.)

During his years as governor, Clinton helped the people of his state. In particular, he worked to improve schools. As time went by, he gained fame across the country. Leaders of

Interesting Facts

▶ In 1988, Clinton
announced that he
would not run for
the presidency in
that year's election.
He said his daughter,
Chelsea, was still a
young child. He
believed it was
important to spend
as much time with
her as possible. He
knew candidates
spend months on the
road, meeting the
American people and
trying to win votes.

the Democratic Party encouraged him to think about running for president. Some expected him to run in 1988, but Clinton decided against it.

Bill Clinton still had his eye on the presidency. In July of 1992, the Democratic Party nominated him as its presidential candidate.

During his first presidential campaign, Bill Clinton often played his saxophone for audiences.

He ran against the incumbent, Republican George Bush. There was also another candidate, H. Ross Perot, from a third political party called the Reform Party.

The presidential campaign of 1992 was difficult. Many Americans were upset by rumors that Clinton had been unfaithful to his wife. The Clintons went on television and admitted that they had had problems in the past. But they said they were happy and vowed to fight together to win the election. They also said they believed their personal life should be private. Millions of voters decided the Clintons' problems did not matter. But some wondered if he was honest enough to hold the country's highest office.

In the months that followed, Clinton gained popularity as he spoke about what he hoped to accomplish if he became president. Many people were worried about the **economy.** Clinton explained how he would work to improve it. He also spoke about his ideas for a new health care system. He wanted the government to help provide quality medical care, especially for people who could not afford insurance. Clinton won the election in November, surprising many people.

President Clinton's first inauguration took place on January 20, 1993. An inauguration is the ceremony that takes place when a new president begins a term.

Bill Clinton's inauguration took place on January 20, 1993. He hoped to make things better for the country. Hillary Rodham Clinton made news headlines early in her husband's term. President Clinton asked her to act as his advisor. This responsibility was very different from those of first ladies in the past. Mrs. Clinton helped the president create a health care plan. She then tried to help him encourage Congress to pass it. In the end, Congress decided it would cost the government too much money. Many felt that the plan tried to do too much, too soon.

In 1994, elections for Congress were held. Republicans won many elections across the country. When they took office the following January, they controlled both houses of Congress, the House of Representatives and the Senate. Clinton had more problems getting **bills** passed with the Republicans in power. He fought with them over the national budget, which determines how the government spends its money. Twice Congress refused to approve the plan Clinton proposed. And twice, the government was forced to shut down because it had no money. Without a budget, the gov-

Chelsea Clinton was 12 years old when her father was elected president. His election meant she began to lead a very public life. Articles appeared about her in newspapers and magazines. Secret Service agents followed her everywhere she went.

ernment cannot dispense money to its programs and its workers. Nearly 300,000 government employees were temporarily laid off. National parks and museums closed. Programs such as Social Security and Meals on Wheels had no money to operate.

Clinton blamed Congress for the shutdown. Most Americans believed he was right. He said many times that it was important for the United States to have a balanced budget, meaning that it should spend only as much as it brought in. Yet some members of Congress wanted to cut **taxes** without reducing spending. By standing up to Congress, Clinton gained the respect of many.

Even though he often fought with Congress, President Clinton did help get important bills passed during his first term. One law cut taxes for small businesses. This helped them compete against larger ones, which had to pay higher taxes. As a result, many people started new small businesses. Another was a gun control law, which made it more difficult to buy guns. Clinton hoped this would help reduce crime. Finally, the Family and Medical Leave Act stated that companies must allow their employees to take time off when they have a new baby or when a member of their family becomes ill.

Clinton had success in relations with other countries as well. His most important achievement was helping to **negotiate** peace between Israel and the Palestinians. Israel, a country in the Middle East, was founded after World War II. To form Israel, land had been taken from the Palestinians and other Arabs in the region. This created terrible problems. For years, a group called the Palestine Liberation Organization fought the Israelis, trying to take back land once owned by Arabs. Clinton's peace talks didn't solve the problems in the Middle East, but many believed it was an important first step.

In 1996, Clinton ran for reelection. This time, his Republican opponent was Senator Bob Dole. Ross Perot entered the race again as well. The economy was an important topic

Clinton was able to sign many important bills during his first four years in office, including the National Voter Registration Act of 1993. This law made it easier for people to register to vote. It also established laws that protected every citizen's right to vote in elections.

once again, but there were new issues as well—including questions about President Clinton's honesty. Early in Clinton's first term, he and Mrs. Clinton had been accused of wrongdoing. Years before, they had invested money in an Arkansas company. Other investors in the company had opened a bank that failed. Reporters wondered whether, as governor of Arkansas, Bill Clinton had used his power to save the bank. A special court asked a lawyer named Kenneth Starr to look into the matter. The situation became known as the Whitewater scandal.

President Clinton had another problem, too. A woman named Paula Jones was **suing** him. She worked for the Arkansas state government. She said that while Clinton was governor of Arkansas, he had pressured her bosses to treat her unfairly after she refused to have sexual relations with him.

Neither the Whitewater scandal nor the Jones lawsuit seemed important to most American citizens. They thought Clinton was doing a good job running the government. The economy was strong, crime was down, and unemployment was lower than it had been in more than 25 years. Clinton was reelected by a large number of votes.

HILLARY RODHAM CLINTON was an active first lady. A smart, educated woman, she graduated from law school at the top of her class. Before her marriage to Bill Clinton, she taught law. Afterward, she began her career as a lawyer. Like her husband, she was always interested in politics. She worked on many presidential campaigns before helping her husband win the elections of 1992 and 1996. During his campaigns, she made public appearances on his behalf. She talked to Americans about the important issues of the day. Americans understood that Mrs. Clinton offered her husband advice and helped him make decisions. After he won the election in 1992, she helped him prepare to become president. Together they chose his closest advisors and the White House staff. Later Mrs. Clinton led the committee charged with creating a national health care plan. She also helped with other important political matters.

In the past, the primary duty of the first lady was to serve as the White House hostess. More recently, first ladies have been more involved in government. Eleanor Roosevelt and Rosalynn Carter are two first ladies who helped their husbands make important political decisions. Hillary Rodham Clinton would take one step they never did, however. In 2000, she ran for political office, winning a seat in the U.S. Senate. Today Americans wonder if she will run for president one day.

Chapter FOUR

Clinton's Trial

President Clinton's second term was troubled by accusations of wrongdoing.

BILL CLINTON BEGAN HIS SECOND TERM IN 1997. He continued to work toward balancing the federal budget. He also wanted to improve the nation's **welfare** system. Another problem would take up much of his time, however. In early 1998, lawyer Kenneth Starr announced publicly that he had begun investigating new charges against President Clinton. Rumors were spreading that Clinton had had an affair with a young worker at the White House. The woman's name was Monica Lewinsky. Clinton had been asked about Lewinsky during the Paula Jones lawsuit. When people are questioned in court, they take an oath in which they swear to tell the truth. If they lie, they are breaking the law. Starr accused Clinton of lying under oath about his relationship with Lewinsky.

In January of 1999, 100 U.S. senators prepared for the historic impeachment trial of President Bill Clinton. They were sworn in by Chief Justice William Rehnquist of the Supreme Court.

On December 19, 1998, the House of Representatives voted to **impeach** Clinton, charging him with lying under oath in court. Being impeached meant Clinton would be tried by the Senate. During the trial, Americans debated whether the president should even be on trial. The U.S. **Constitution** says impeachment is the process used to determine whether presidents have committed "high crimes and **misdemeanors.**" Clinton's political supporters agreed that he had done something wrong in his personal life, but said that it had not affected his job as president. Those against Clinton said that he was a man of bad character and that he had broken the law by lying under oath. They believed he must be punished by being removed from office.

Interesting Facts

▸ When Clinton was reelected in 1996, he became the first president from the Democratic Party to win a second term since Franklin D. Roosevelt 60 years before.

33

The American people talked a great deal about the trial. Many thought that even though President Clinton broke the law when he lied under oath, he should not be removed from office. **Polls** taken by newspapers and television networks revealed that people still believed Clinton was doing a good job. Many believed the trial was a sign of the terrible relations between Democrats and Republicans in the government.

The impeachment trial continued into February of 1999. When the Senate voted on whether to convict the president, less than half of the senators voted to remove him from office. This was less than the two-thirds vote required by the Constitution. Clinton would remain the president. By that time, polls showed that most Americans did not consider him to be an honest man. Even so, he remained a popular president. Americans felt confident in his ability to lead the nation. Clinton was grateful to have a second chance.

After his impeachment trial, Clinton devoted his attention to foreign affairs. He and his aides organized peace talks to help end a war in Bosnia, a small European country that was formerly part of Yugoslavia. He also worked to bring peace to Northern Ireland. Toward the end of Clinton's presidency, the American military was involved in a war in Kosovo, part of the Federal Republic of Yugoslavia. Enemy soldiers had invaded this tiny region. The United States and its **allies** bombed these forces to make them leave Kosovo.

The U.S. Constitution says presidents can serve only two terms, so Clinton could not run for reelection in 2000. His wife, however, ran for the Senate and won. Clinton's vice president, Al Gore, ran in the presidential election that year. George W. Bush, son of the 41st president, ran as the Republican candidate. The election was extremely close. For weeks, it remained unclear who had won. Finally, George W. Bush was declared the winner.

As the end of Clinton's presidency neared, he remained hard at work. He continued to work for peace in the Middle East, a goal he

Polls showed that most Americans did not want Congress to impeach President Clinton, even though many believed he was not an honest person. Protesters appeared in Washington, D.C., to show their support for him.

President Clinton gave his farewell address on January 18, 2001. He thanked the country for his eight years in office and wished president-elect George W. Bush well.

had hoped to achieve throughout his presidency. He also tried to create laws to help the environment.

On his last day in office, Clinton issued a statement in which he admitted that he had broken the law when he lied under oath. Because of this, his law license was taken away for five years. This means he could not work as a lawyer during that time. But in exchange for his statement, officials announced that Clinton would not face another trial for what he had done.

When he left office, Clinton expressed pride in his accomplishments as president. "I am grateful to be able to turn over the reins of leadership to a new president, with America in a great position to meet the challenges of the future," he said to Americans in his farewell address. "Working together, America has done well." Whatever the future holds for Bill Clinton, he is sure to set new goals for himself. Although people will remember the impeachment and the questions about his character, they will also remember the good that came from his presidency.

WHEN THE UNITED STATES WAS A NEW NATION, THE MEN WHO WROTE THE U.S. Constitution understood that someday a president might be involved in a crime. Or, that the president might do something so wrong that he (or she) should no longer remain in office. The Constitution gives Congress the power to 1. impeach the president, 2. put him or her on trial, 3. convict him or her, and 4. remove the president from office. This is how the impeachment process works:

1. According to the Constitution, if a majority of members of the House of Representatives vote that they believe the president has committed "treason, bribery, or other high crimes and misdemeanors," then they have impeached the president. Two presidents have been impeached, Andrew Johnson in 1868 and Bill Clinton in 1998. Neither was found guilty of a crime. In 1974, President Richard Nixon **resigned** before the House voted whether to impeach him.

2. Once the House has impeached the president, the Senate must put the him or her on trial. During the trial, the Senate hears evidence of the president's wrongdoing. The president's lawyers defend his or her actions. Then the senators vote. If two-thirds or more of the senators vote to convict the president, then he or she must be removed from office. If fewer than two-thirds of the senators vote to convict, the president is acquitted and remains in office. (The Constitution also allows Congress to impeach the vice president and other "civil officers of the United States." Civil officers include judges and other important government officials.)

1946 William Jefferson Blythe is born on August 19. His mother is Virginia Blythe. His father, William Jefferson Blythe Sr., had died in a car accident three months before.

1963 Clinton makes his first trip to Washington, D.C. As a participant in Boys Nation, he meets President John F. Kennedy.

1964 After graduating from high school, Clinton enrolls at Georgetown University, in Washington, D.C.

1968 During his final year of college, Clinton wins a Rhodes Scholarship. He travels to England to study at Oxford University.

1970 Clinton returns home from England and enrolls at Yale Law School.

1973 After earning his law degree, Clinton becomes a professor of law at the University of Arkansas.

1974 Clinton runs for election for the first time, hoping to win a seat in the U.S. House of Representatives. He loses to the incumbent.

1975 Clinton marries Hillary Rodham on October 11.

1976 Clinton wins election as attorney general of Arkansas.

1978 Clinton is elected governor of Arkansas.

1980 The Clintons' only child, Chelsea, is born. Bill Clinton runs for reelection as governor but loses.

1981 Clinton starts a new job as an attorney. He spends much of his time building political support so he can run for election as governor again.

1982 Clinton is again elected governor of Arkansas.

1988 Democrats hope Clinton will run for president, but he decides against it.

1992 Clinton wins election as president of the United States, beating Republican George Bush, the incumbent.

1993 Clinton is inaugurated on January 20. He is disappointed when Congress refuses to agree to his plan for a national health care program. An investigation begins into the Whitewater scandal, a business deal in which the Clintons were involved years before. An historic peace agreement between Israel and the Palestine Liberation Organization is signed at the White House.

1994 Republicans win many elections and gain control of both the House of Representatives and the Senate. From this time on, Clinton must fight even harder to get bills passed.

1995 Clinton and Congress fight over the national budget. Clinton hosts peace talks between the groups that have been fighting in Bosnia, formerly part of Yugoslavia. A new Middle East peace agreement is signed, but fighting continues.

1996 In November, Clinton wins reelection to a second term as president.

1997 Kenneth Starr, the government's lawyer, continues to investigate the Whitewater scandal. He begins to investigate whether President Clinton had lied under oath.

1998 New fighting breaks out in the Federal Republic of Yugoslavia when Kosovo is invaded. Iraqi President Saddam Hussein breaks his promise to let United Nations inspectors confirm that Iraq is not building chemical weapons and nuclear arms. President Clinton authorizes the American military to bomb Iraq. In December, Clinton is impeached on charges of perjury and obstruction of justice by the House of Representatives.

1999 The Senate tries Bill Clinton. On February 12, senators vote on whether to convict him on the articles of impeachment. Not enough senators vote to remove him, and he stays in office. After having failed to negotiate peace in Kosovo, Clinton orders the American military to join U.S. allies in the bombing of the invaders. Bombing ends in June, when a peace plan is reached.

2000 Clinton continues to work with Israeli and Palestinian leaders to reach a peace agreement, but trouble in the Middle East continues. Having served two terms, Clinton cannot run in the November presidential election. His vice president, Al Gore, runs against George W. Bush. The election is extremely close, and the outcome takes weeks to be decided. In December, Republican George W. Bush is determined to be the winner.

2001 Bill Clinton leaves office when George W. Bush is inaugurated the 43rd president on January 20.

Glossary TERMS

allies (AL-lize)
Allies are nations that have agreed to help each other by fighting against a common enemy. In 1999, the United States and its allies bombed enemy forces that invaded Kosovo.

assassinate (uh-SASS-ih-nayt)
Assassinate means to murder someone, especially a well-known person. Martin Luther King Jr. was assassinated in 1968.

bills (BILZ)
Bills are ideas for new laws that are presented to a group of lawmakers. Because there were so many Republicans in Congress, Clinton had trouble getting his bills passed.

campaign (kam-PAYN)
A campaign is the process of running for an election, including activities such as giving speeches or attending rallies. In the summer of 1966, Clinton took part in his first political campaign.

candidate (KAN-dih-det)
A candidate is a person running in an election. While at Yale, Clinton worked for the Democratic presidential candidate, George McGovern.

**Civil Rights Movement
(SIV-el RYTZ MOOV-ment)**
The Civil Rights Movement was the name given to the struggle for equal rights for African Americans in the United States during the 1950s and 1960s. Clinton was interested in the Civil Rights Movement as a young man.

communists (KOM-yeh-nists)
Communists are people who support a system of government called communism. In this system, the government, not the people, holds all the power, and there is no private ownership of property.

conserve (kun-SERV)
If people conserve something, they save or do not waste it. As attorney general of Arkansas, Clinton tried to make utility companies conserve energy.

constitution (kon-stih-TOO-shun)
A constitution is the set of basic principles that govern a state, country, or society. The U.S. Constitution includes laws about the impeachment process.

drafted (DRAF-ted)
When people are drafted, they are required by law to join the military. During the Vietnam War, thousands of young American men were drafted into the military.

economy (ee-KON-uh-mee)
An economy is the way money is earned and spent. During his 1992 campaign, Clinton promised to improve the U.S. economy.

impeach (im-PEECH)
If the House of Representatives votes to impeach a president, it charges him or her with a crime or serious misdeed. Clinton was the second president to be impeached.

incumbent (in-KUM-bent)
An incumbent is the person who currently holds an elected office. Clinton lost his first election to the incumbent.

misdemeanors (mis-deh-MEE-nurz)
Misdemeanors are wrongful actions (such as lying under oath) that are less serious than heavier crimes (such as murder). Impeachment is the process used to determine whether presidents have committed "high crimes and misdemeanors."

negotiate (neh-GOH-shee-ayt)
If people negotiate, they talk things over and try to come to an agreement. Clinton tried to negotiate peace between Israel and the Palestinians.

**political parties
(puh-LIT-ih-kul PAR-teez)**
Political parties are groups of people who share similar ideas about how to run a government. The Democratic and Republican parties are the two largest political parties in the United States.

politician (pawl-ih-TISH-un)
A politician is a person who holds an office in government. Many people considered Bill Clinton a great politician.

politics (PAWL-ih-tiks)
Politics refers to the actions and practices of the government. As a young man, politics fascinated Clinton.

polls (POHLZ)
Polls are surveys of people's opinions on subjects. During Clinton's impeachment trial, polls showed that Americans still believed he was doing a good job.

resign (ree-ZINE)
When a person resigns from a job, he or she gives it up. President Richard Nixon resigned from office before the House of Representatives voted whether to impeach him.

scandal (SKAN-dul)
A scandal is a shameful action that shocks the public. When the government investigated a business deal of the Clintons', it became known as the Whitewater scandal.

sue (SOO)
When people sue, they take another person to court to resolve a disagreement. During the 1996 election, Paula Jones was suing President Clinton.

taxes (TAK-sez)
Taxes are payments of money made by citizens to support a government. Some members of Congress wanted to cut taxes without reducing spending during Clinton's presidency.

term (TERM)
A term is the period of time a politician can hold a position by law. A U.S. president's term is four years.

United Nations (yoo-NY-ted NAY-shunz)
The United Nations is an international organization made up of more than 180 countries. It was founded to end war and achieve world peace.

welfare (WELL-fair)
Welfare is aid provided by the government to poor or needy people. Clinton wanted to improve the nation's welfare system.

Our PRESIDENTS

President	Birthplace	Life Span	Presidency	Political Party	First Lady
George Washington	Virginia	1732–1799	1789–1797	None	Martha Dandridge Custis Washington
John Adams	Massachusetts	1735–1826	1797–1801	Federalist	Abigail Smith Adams
Thomas Jefferson	Virginia	1743–1826	1801–1809	Democratic-Republican	widower
James Madison	Virginia	1751–1836	1809–1817	Democratic Republican	Dolley Payne Todd Madison
James Monroe	Virginia	1758–1831	1817–1825	Democratic Republican	Elizabeth Kortright Monroe
John Quincy Adams	Massachusetts	1767–1848	1825–1829	Democratic-Republican	Louisa Johnson Adams
Andrew Jackson	South Carolina	1767–1845	1829–1837	Democrat	widower
Martin Van Buren	New York	1782–1862	1837–1841	Democrat	widower
William H. Harrison	Virginia	1773–1841	1841	Whig	Anna Symmes Harrison
John Tyler	Virginia	1790–1862	1841–1845	Whig	Letitia Christian Tyle Julia Gardiner Tyler
James K. Polk	North Carolina	1795–1849	1845–1849	Democrat	Sarah Childress Polk

Our PRESENTS

President	Birthplace	Life Span	Presidency	Political Party	First Lady
Zachary Taylor	Virginia	1784–1850	1849–1850	Whig	Margaret Mackall Smith Taylor
Millard Fillmore	New York	1800–1874	1850–1853	Whig	Abigail Powers Fillmore
Franklin Pierce	New Hampshire	1804–1869	1853–1857	Democrat	Jane Means Appleton Pierce
James Buchanan	Pennsylvania	1791–1868	1857–1861	Democrat	never married
Abraham Lincoln	Kentucky	1809–1865	1861–1865	Republican	Mary Todd Lincoln
Andrew Johnson	North Carolina	1808–1875	1865–1869	Democrat	Eliza McCardle Johnson
Ulysses S. Grant	Ohio	1822–1885	1869–1877	Republican	Julia Dent Grant
Rutherford B. Hayes	Ohio	1822–1893	1877–1881	Republican	Lucy Webb Hayes
James A. Garfield	Ohio	1831–1881	1881	Republican	Lucretia Rudolph Garfield
Chester A. Arthur	Vermont	1829–1886	1881–1885	Republican	widower
Grover Cleveland	New Jersey	1837–1908	1885–1889	Democrat	Frances Folsom Cleveland

President	Birthplace	Life Span	Presidency	Political Party	First Lady
Benjamin Harrison	Ohio	1833–1901	1889–1893	Republican	Caroline Scott Harrison
Grover Cleveland	New Jersey	1837–1908	1893–1897	Democrat	Frances Folsom Cleveland
William McKinley	Ohio	1843–1901	1897–1901	Republican	Ida Saxton McKinley
Theodore Roosevelt	New York	1858–1919	1901–1909	Republican	Edith Kermit Carow Roosevelt
William H. Taft	Ohio	1857–1930	1909–1913	Republican	Helen Herron Taft
Woodrow Wilson	Virginia	1856–1924	1913–1921	Democrat	Ellen L. Axson Wilson Edith Bolling Galt Wilson
Warren G. Harding	Ohio	1865–1923	1921–1923	Republican	Florence Kling De Wolfe Harding
Calvin Coolidge	Vermont	1872–1933	1923–1929	Republican	Grace Goodhue Coolidge
Herbert C. Hoover	Iowa	1874–1964	1929–1933	Republican	Lou Henry Hoover
Franklin D. Roosevelt	New York	1882–1945	1933–1945	Democrat	Anna Eleanor Roosevelt Roosevelt
Harry S. Truman	Missouri	1884–1972	1945–1953	Democrat	Elizabeth Wallace Truman

President	Birthplace	Life Span	Presidency	Political Party	First Lady
Dwight D. Eisenhower	Texas	1890–1969	1953–1961	Republican	Mary "Mamie" Doud Eisenhower
John F. Kennedy	Massachusetts	1917–1963	1961–1963	Democrat	Jacqueline Bouvier Kennedy
Lyndon B. Johnson	Texas	1908–1973	1963–1969	Democrat	Claudia Alta Taylor Johnson
Richard M. Nixon	California	1913–1994	1969–1974	Republican	Thelma Catherine Ryan Nixon
Gerald Ford	Nebraska	1913–	1974–1977	Republican	Elizabeth "Betty" Bloomer Warren Ford
James Carter	Georgia	1924–	1977–1981	Democrat	Rosalynn Smith Carter
Ronald Reagan	Illinois	1911–	1981–1989	Republican	Nancy Davis Reagan
George Bush	Massachusetts	1924–	1989–1993	Republican	Barbara Pierce Bush
William Clinton	Arkansas	1946–	1993–2001	Democrat	Hillary Rodham Clinton
George W. Bush	Connecticut	1946–	2001–	Republican	Laura Welch Bush

Qualifications

To run for president, a candidate must
- be at least 35 years old
- be a citizen who was born in the United States
- have lived in the United States for 14 years

Term of Office

A president's term of office is four years. No president can stay in office for more than two terms.

Election Date

The presidential election takes place every four years on the first Tuesday of November.

Inauguration Date

Presidents are inaugurated on January 20.

Oath of Office

I do solemnly swear I will faithfully execute the office of the President of the United States and will to the best of my ability preserve, protect, and defend the Constitution of the United States.

Write a Letter to the President

One of the best things about being a U.S. citizen is that Americans get to participate in their government. They can speak out if they feel government leaders aren't doing their jobs. They can also praise leaders who are going the extra mile. Do you have something you'd like the president to do? Should the president worry more about the environment and encourage people to recycle? Should the government spend more money on our schools? You can write a letter to the president to say how you feel!

1600 Pennsylvania Avenue
Washington, D.C. 20500

You can even send an e-mail to: president@whitehouse.gov

For Further INFORMATION

Internet Sites

Visit an exhibit about Bill Clinton at Hot Springs National Park:
http://www.hsnp.com/clinton.html

Learn more about Hillary Rodham Clinton:
www.wic.org/bio/hclinton.htm

Learn more about President Clinton and his two terms in office:
http://www.facts.com/cd/b00007.htm
http://www.potus.com/wjclinton.html

Read *Time* magazine's coverage of the impeachment trial:
http://www.time.com/time/daily/scandal/

Read President Clinton's inaugural addresses:
http://www.bartleby.com/124/pres64.html
http://www.bartleby.com/124/pres65.html

Learn more about all the presidents and visit the White House:
http://www.whitehouse.gov/WH/glimpse/presidents/html/presidents.html
http://www.thepresidency.org/presinfo.htm
http://www.americanpresidents.org/

Books

Cohen, Daniel. *Impeachment of William Jefferson Clinton.* New York: Twenty-First Century Books, 2000.

Cwiklik, Robert. *Bill Clinton: President of the 90s.* Brookfield, CT: Millbrook Press, 1997.

Greenberg, Keith Elliot. *Bill & Hillary: Working Together.* Woodbridge, CT: Blackbirch Press, 1994.

Maraniss, David. *First in His Class: A Biography of Bill Clinton.* New York: Simon & Schuster, 1995.

Index